No Bulling Around with MQL5 MetaTrader Programming

By: Michael Neumann

No Bulling Around with MQL5 MetaTrader Programming

By: Michael Neumann

Published by Mediaguruz Publishing at Mediaguruz.com

Table of Contents

Chapter 1: Introduction to MQL5 and Automated Trading

Overview of MQL5

MetaQuotes Language 5 (MQL5) is an advanced programming language for developing trading strategies, indicators, scripts, and function libraries within the MetaTrader 5 (MT5) trading platform. MQL5 is designed specifically for automating trading activities and conducting technical analysis in real-time.

Key Features:

- **High Performance**: MQL5 is faster and more efficient, handling complex calculations and data analysis with ease.

- **Advanced Event-Driven Architecture**: The language's event-driven model allows scripts to respond to market changes instantaneously.

- **Built-In Expert Advisors (EAs)**: MQL5 facilitates the creation of EAs for automated trading.

- **Integration with C++ Libraries**: MQL5 supports integration with external libraries, enhancing its functionality.

Differences between MQL4 and MQL5

While MQL4 and MQL5 are similar in syntax, there are significant differences:

- **Execution Speed**: MQL5 is faster due to its multi-threaded, multi-currency, and real-time testing capabilities.

- **Object-Oriented Programming (OOP)**: MQL5 fully supports OOP, offering better organization and more robust development capabilities.

- **Advanced Debugging and Testing**: MQL5 provides more sophisticated tools for debugging and strategy testing.

- **Graphical Objects**: Enhanced graphical capabilities in MQL5 allow for more dynamic and interactive chart objects.

Setting up the MetaTrader 5 Environment

To start using MQL5, you need to set up the MT5 platform:

1. **Download and Install MetaTrader 5**: Available for free from most online brokers or the official MetaQuotes website.

2. **Navigate the MT5 Interface**: Familiarize yourself with the interface, focusing on the Market Watch, Navigator, and Terminal windows.

3. **Open the MetaEditor**: This is the integrated development environment (IDE) for MQL5, where you will write and compile your scripts.

Example: Hello World in MQL5

```
void OnStart()

{

Print("Hello, World!");

}
```

Basic Concepts of Automated Trading

Automated trading involves using algorithms (EAs in MT5) to make trading decisions and place orders automatically.

Components:

Expert Advisors (EAs): Programs that automate trading and analytical tasks on MT5.

Definition:

- **Expert Advisors (EAs)** are automated trading programs developed using the MQL5 programming language. They run on the MT5 platform and can execute trades on behalf of traders following a predefined trading strategy.

Key Characteristics:

- **Automated Trading**: EAs can open, modify, and close trades automatically, based on their programmed strategy.

- **Customizable**: Traders can create EAs tailored to their specific trading rules, risk tolerance, and strategies.

- **Backtesting Capability**: EAs can be tested against historical data in MT5 to evaluate their effectiveness before actual trading.

- **Event-Driven**: They react to market events in real-time, ensuring timely execution of trades.

Example Usage:

```
// Simple Moving Average EA example
input int fastMAPeriod = 10; // Fast MA period
input int slowMAPeriod = 20; // Slow MA period

void OnTick()
{
    double fastMA = iMA(Symbol(), Period(), fastMAPeriod, 0, MODE_SMA,
PRICE_CLOSE, 0);
    double slowMA = iMA(Symbol(), Period(), slowMAPeriod, 0, MODE_SMA,
PRICE_CLOSE, 0);

    if(fastMA > slowMA)
    {
        // Logic for opening a buy order
    }
    else if(fastMA < slowMA)
    {
        // Logic for opening a sell order
    }
}
```

Indicators: Tools used to analyze market trends and conditions.

Definition:

- **Indicators** are tools used in technical analysis to predict future market trends and conditions based on historical price data. They are used to create trading signals or to identify the market state.

Key Characteristics:

- **Variety of Types**: Includes trend indicators (like Moving Averages), momentum indicators (like RSI), volume indicators, and more.
- **Custom Indicators**: Traders can develop their own custom indicators in MQL5 for specific analysis needs.
- **Visual Representation**: Typically represented graphically on the trading chart, making it easier to interpret market data.

Example Usage:

```
// Example: Calculating Simple Moving Average
double SMA = iMA(Symbol(), Period(), 14, 0, MODE_SMA, PRICE_CLOSE, 0);
```

Scripts: Used for single-shot tasks like placing an order or closing all positions.

Definition:

- **Scripts** in MQL5 are programs that are designed to perform a single action. Unlike EAs, they do not run continuously or react to market events.

Key Characteristics:

- **One-Time Execution**: Scripts execute their code once and then terminate. They're used for tasks like placing an order or closing all positions.
- **Simplicity**: Generally simpler than EAs, as they are meant for specific tasks.
- **No Strategy Implementation**: Unlike EAs, scripts are not used for implementing trading strategies.

Example Usage:

```
// Example: Script to close all open positions
void OnStart()
{
    for(int i = PositionsTotal()-1; i >= 0; i--)
    {
        ulong ticket = PositionGetTicket(i);
        if(PositionSelectByTicket(ticket))
        {
// Logic to close the position
        }
    }
}
```

Advantages:

- **Speed and Efficiency**: Automated systems can process information and execute trades much faster than humans.

- **Emotion-Free Trading**: Removes emotional biases from trading decisions.

- **Backtesting**: EAs can be tested on historical data to refine strategies.

Risks and Considerations:

- **Market Unpredictability**: Automated systems may not effectively handle unexpected market events.

- **Technical Failures**: System malfunctions can lead to missed opportunities or losses.

- **Over-Optimization**: EAs might be over-tuned to past market conditions and may not perform well in the future.

In summary, EAs, indicators, and scripts are powerful tools provided by MT5 for automating trading and analysis. EAs automate complex trading strategies and can operate continuously, indicators assist in technical analysis and decision-making, and scripts are perfect for executing one-time tasks such as trade modifications or account management. Understanding these components is essential for anyone looking to leverage the full capabilities of the MT5 platform.

Chapter 2: Understanding MetaTrader 5 Platform

Navigating the MT5 Interface

Overview:

- MetaTrader 5 (MT5) is a powerful trading platform known for its comprehensive tools and intuitive interface. It caters to traders of all levels, from beginners to advanced professionals.

Key Components of the Interface:

- **Market Watch**: This section displays a list of financial instruments, their prices, spreads, and other essential trading information.

- **Navigator**: Provides quick access to accounts, indicators, Expert Advisors (EAs), and scripts.

- **Terminal**: Shows account balance, open positions, order history, and allows management of trades.

- **Toolbar**: Contains shortcuts to commonly used tools and functions for charting and analysis.

Navigating Tips:

- Utilize the 'drag and drop' feature to easily apply indicators or EAs to charts.
- Customize the layout and profiles for different trading strategies or instruments.

Key Features and Tools

Trading and Order Execution:

- **One-Click Trading**: A feature for fast order execution right from the chart.

- **Multiple Order Types**: MT5 supports various order types, including market orders, pending orders, stop orders, and a trailing stop.

Analytical Tools:

- **Technical Indicators**: MT5 comes with 38 built-in indicators for comprehensive technical analysis.

- **Graphical Objects**: Over 44 graphical objects are available for detailed chart analysis.

Algorithmic Trading:

- **Expert Advisors (EAs)**: Automate trading using custom EAs.

- **MQL5 Development Environment**: Develop and test custom EAs, indicators, and scripts.

Fundamental Analysis:

- **Economic Calendar**: Integrated calendar for tracking important financial events and news releases.

- **Financial News**: Stay updated with real-time financial news within the platform.

Understanding MT5 Charting and Analysis

Chart Setup:

- MT5 offers multi-chart setups, allowing traders to monitor multiple instruments simultaneously.
- Customize chart types (e.g., bar, candlestick, line) and time frames according to trading needs.

Applying Technical Indicators:

- Easily apply indicators like Moving Averages, MACD, RSI, etc., to charts for analysis.
- Customize indicator parameters to fit specific strategies.

Graphical Analysis Tools:

- Use tools like trendlines, channels, Fibonacci retracements for graphical analysis.
- Modify and save graphical object properties for future use.

Example of Setting Up a Chart for Analysis:

1. Open the 'Market Watch' window, right-click on the desired instrument, and select 'Chart Window'.

2. Choose a time frame (e.g., H1 for one-hour candles) from the toolbar.

3. Select 'Insert' from the menu, navigate to 'Indicators', and choose an indicator like 'Bollinger Bands'.

4. Customize the indicator settings in the pop-up window and click 'OK'.

5. Add graphical objects like trendlines by selecting them from the toolbar and applying them directly to the chart.

Conclusion

Understanding the MT5 platform is essential for efficient and effective trading. Familiarity with its interface, tools, and charting capabilities empowers traders to analyze the markets thoroughly and execute trades confidently. Whether you are a beginner or an experienced trader, mastering the functionalities of MT5 is a crucial step in your trading journey. This chapter provides a solid foundation for navigating and utilizing the MetaTrader 5 platform to its full potential.

Chapter 3: Basics of MQL5 Programming

Syntax and Structure

General Syntax:

- MQL5 is a high-level programming language that shares many syntactical similarities with C++.

- It follows a clear and structured syntax, making the code readable and maintainable.

Basic Program Structure:

- A typical MQL5 program consists of predefined functions like **OnInit()**, **OnTick()**, and **OnDeinit()** that the MT5 platform calls.

- **OnInit()**: Called when the script, EA, or indicator is initialized.

- **OnTick()**: For EAs, this function is called on every new tick of price data.

- **OnDeinit()**: Called when the script, EA, or indicator is removed or MT5 is closed.

Commenting Code:

- Single-line comments are initiated with **//**, and multi-line comments start with **/*** and end with ***/**.

Variables and Data Types

Understanding Variables:

- Variables are placeholders or containers for storing data values.
- In MQL5, variables must be declared with a specific data type before they are used.

Common Data Types:

- **int**: For integers.
- **double**: For floating-point numbers.
- **string**: For text.
- **bool**: For Boolean values (**true** or **false**).
- **datetime**: For date and time.

Declaration and Initialization:

```
int lots = 1;      // Integer

double price = 1.5; // Floating-point number

string name = "EURUSD"; // String

bool isTrading = true;  // Boolean

datetime openTime;      // Date and time
```

Operators and Expressions

Arithmetic Operators:

- Used for basic mathematical operations: + (addition), - (subtraction), * (multiplication), / (division), and % (modulus).

Relational Operators:

- For comparing values: == (equal to), != (not equal to), > (greater than), < (less than), >= (greater than or equal to), <= (less than or equal to).

Logical Operators:

- Used to form compound conditions: && (logical AND), || (logical OR), ! (logical NOT).

Example Code: Simple Calculations

Objective:

- Create a simple script to demonstrate basic arithmetic operations and variable usage.

```
void OnStart()
{
  // Declare and initialize variables
  double priceBuy = 1.1350;
  double priceSell = 1.1380;

  // Calculate the difference
  double spread = priceSell - priceBuy;

  // Output the result
  Print("The spread is: ", spread);
}
```

Explanation:

- This script calculates the spread based on buy and sell prices.

- Variables **priceBuy** and **priceSell** are initialized with prices.

- The arithmetic operation (subtraction) is performed and stored in the **spread** variable.

- The result is printed to the MT5 logs using the **Print()** function.

Chapter 4: Control Structures in MQL5

Control structures are fundamental in any programming language, including MQL5, as they allow you to control the flow of execution based on certain conditions or iterations. In this chapter, we'll explore the essential control structures in MQL5: conditional statements and loops. Understanding these concepts is key to creating dynamic and responsive trading algorithms.

Conditional Statements

Purpose:

- Conditional statements allow the program to execute different code blocks based on specific conditions.

Types:

1. **If-Else Statements**: The most common form of conditional logic in MQL5.

   Syntax:

   ```
   if (condition) {
       // code to execute if condition is true
   } else {
       // code to execute if condition is false
   }
   ```

- Used for making decisions in the code, like executing a trade under certain market conditions.

2. **Switch Statements**: Useful for executing different blocks of code based on the value of a variable.

Syntax:

```
switch (expression) {
case value1:
    // code block
    break;
case value2:
    // code block
    break;
default:
    // default code block
}
```

Loops and Iteration

Purpose:

- Loops are used to execute a block of code repeatedly, either a set number of times or until a certain condition is met.

Types:

For Loop: Executes a block of code a specific number of times.

Syntax:

```
for (initialization; condition; increment) {
  // code block to be executed
}
```

- Commonly used for iterating over arrays or repetitive tasks.

While Loop: Repeats a block of code as long as a specified condition is true.

Syntax:

```
while (condition) {
  // code block to be executed
}
```

Do-While Loop: Similar to the while loop, but the code block is executed at least once before the condition is tested.

Syntax:

```
do {
// code block to be executed
} while (condition);
```

Example Code: Implementing a Conditional Trading Logic

Objective:

- Create a simple Expert Advisor (EA) that uses conditional statements to decide when to execute trades.

Example Script:

```
//-------------------------------------------------------------------
// Simple Moving Average Crossover EA
//-------------------------------------------------------------------
input int fastMAPeriod = 10; // Fast Moving Average Period
input int slowMAPeriod = 20; // Slow Moving Average Period


//-------------------------------------------------------------------
 Expert tick function                              |
//-------------------------------------------------------------------
void OnTick()
  {
   // Calculate Moving Averages
   double fastMA = iMA(Symbol(), Period(), fastMAPeriod, 0, MODE_SMA, PRICE_CLOSE, 0);
   double slowMA = iMA(Symbol(), Period(), slowMAPeriod, 0, MODE_SMA, PRICE_CLOSE, 0);


   // Trading logic
   if(fastMA > slowMA && OrdersTotal() == 0)
     {
      // If fast MA crosses above slow MA and no open orders, place a buy order
```

```
        OrderSend(Symbol(), OP_BUY, 0.1, Ask, 2, 0, 0, "Buy Order", 0, clrNONE);

    }

    else if(fastMA < slowMA && OrdersTotal() == 0)

    {

        // If fast MA crosses below slow MA and no open orders, place a sell order

        OrderSend(Symbol(), OP_SELL, 0.1, Bid, 2, 0, 0, "Sell Order", 0, clrNONE);

    }

}
//-------------------------------------------------------------------
```

Explanation:

- The script uses two moving averages (fast and slow) to determine the market trend.

- The **if-else** statements control whether to place a buy or sell order based on the crossover of these moving averages.

- The script also checks if there are no open orders before placing a new one, using a conditional check **OrdersTotal() == 0**.

In this chapter, we have laid the foundation for controlling the flow of execution in MQL5 scripts. By mastering conditional statements and loops, you can develop sophisticated trading algorithms that react dynamically to market conditions. The example provided illustrates how these concepts can be applied in practical trading scenarios.

Chapter 5: Functions and Event Handlers

Defining and Calling Functions

Introduction to Functions:

- Functions are self-contained blocks of code designed to perform a specific task.
- They can receive input parameters, process them, and return a result.

Defining a Function:

- A function is defined with a return type, a unique name, and an optional list of parameters.

- MQL5 supports various return types, including basic types like **int**, **double**, **string**, and complex types like custom classes.

Syntax:

```
return_type FunctionName(parameter1_type parameter1, parameter2_type parameter2)

{

// Function code

    return value; // If the function has a return type

}
```

Calling a Function:

Functions are called by their name, with necessary parameters passed as arguments.

Example of Function Definition and Call:

```
// Function to calculate the average of two numbers
double Average(double num1, double num2)
{
    return (num1 + num2) / 2;
}


// Calling the function
void OnStart()
{
    double result = Average(10, 20);
    Print("Average: ", result);
}
```

Understanding Event Handlers in MQL5

Role of Event Handlers:

Event handlers in MQL5 are special functions that are automatically called by the MT5 platform in response to specific events.

Key Event Handlers:

- **OnInit():** Called when an EA or indicator is initialized.
- **OnTick():** For EAs, called on every new price tick.
- **OnTimer():** Called when a timer event occurs.
- **OnTrade():** Triggered when a trade event (like a position opening or closing) occurs.

Event Handler Characteristics:

- They must be included in your script if you need to respond to their respective events.
- Each event handler has a specific predefined name and structure.

Example Code: Writing a Custom Function for Indicators

Objective:

- Create a custom function to calculate a simple moving average, demonstrating function usage in the context of market analysis.

Example Script:

```
// Function to calculate Simple Moving Average
double CalculateSMA(int period, int shift)
{
    double total = 0.0;


    for(int i = shift; i < period + shift; i++)
    {
        total += Close[i];
    }


    return total / period;
```

```
}
```

```
// Using the custom function in the OnTick() event handler

void OnTick()

{

    double sma = CalculateSMA(14, 0); // 14-period SMA

    Print("Current SMA: ", sma);

}
```

Explanation:

- The **CalculateSMA** function computes the simple moving average for a given period and shift on the current chart.
- It loops through the closing prices of the last 'period' bars, accumulates their total, and then divides by the 'period' to get the average.
- This function is then called within the **OnTick** event handler to calculate and print the 14-period SMA whenever a new tick is received.

The ability to write custom functions and properly handle events opens up vast possibilities for developing sophisticated and efficient trading strategies and scripts in MT5. The provided example showcases how these concepts can be practically applied in creating custom indicators or EAs.

Chapter 6: Working with Time and Date

Time and date management is a critical aspect of automated trading systems. In MQL5, various functions and features allow traders to effectively handle time-based data and events. This chapter explores the essential date and time functions in MQL5, the use of timers, and how to manage events based on time. We'll conclude with an example demonstrating time-based trade execution.

Date and Time Functions

Understanding Time in MQL5:

- MQL5 provides several functions to handle date and time, crucial for tasks like timing trade orders or analyzing market movements over time.

Common Time Functions:

1. **TimeCurrent()**: Returns the current server time.
2. **TimeLocal()**: Provides the current local time of the computer.
3. **TimeDayOfWeek()**: Returns the day of the week for a given time.
4. **TimeDayOfYear()**: Provides the day of the year.
5. **TimeToStruct()**: Converts a datetime value to a MqlDateTime structure for easy handling.

Using MqlDateTime:

- The **MqlDateTime** structure breaks down a datetime value into year, month, day, hour, minute, and second, making it easier to work with.

Example of Time Function:

```
datetime currentTime = TimeCurrent();

MqlDateTime structTime;

TimeToStruct(currentTime, structTime);


Print("Current Time: ", structTime.hour, ":", structTime.minute, ":", structTime.second);
```

Timers and Event Handling Based on Time

Timers in MQL5:

- Timers allow you to execute code at specific intervals.
- Use the **EventSetTimer()** and **EventKillTimer()** functions to manage timers.

Handling the OnTimer() Event:

- The **OnTimer()** event handler is triggered at intervals set by **EventSetTimer()**.
- Useful for actions that need to be executed periodically but not on every tick.

Example of Setting a Timer:

```
void OnInit()
{
    // Set a timer to trigger every 5 seconds
    EventSetTimer(5);
}


void OnTimer()
{
    // Code to be executed every 5 seconds
    Print("Timer triggered at ", TimeToStr(TimeCurrent(), TIME_SECONDS));
}


void OnDeinit(const int reason)
{
    // Kill the timer when the script is removed
    EventKillTimer();
}
```

Example Code: Time-Based Trade Execution

Objective:

- Create an EA that executes a trade at a specific time of day.

Example Script:

```
input int tradeHour = 15; // Trade at 3 PM server time
void OnTick()
{

   MqlDateTime currentTime;
   TimeToStruct(TimeCurrent(), currentTime);

   // Check if it's the specific hour and no open orders
   if(currentTime.hour == tradeHour && OrdersTotal() == 0)
   {
     // Trade execution logic
       double price = SymbolInfoDouble(_Symbol, SYMBOL_BID);
       OrderSend(_Symbol, OP_SELL, 0.1, price, 2, 0, 0, "Sell Order", 0, clrRed);
   }

}
```

Explanation:

- The script checks the current server time every tick.
- If it matches the specified trade hour (**'tradeHour'**) and there are no open orders, it executes a trade.
- This approach is useful for strategies that rely on trading at specific times, such as market openings or after economic announcements.

Chapter 7: Advanced Data Types and Collections

Arrays and Structures

Arrays in MQL5:

- **Definition**: An array is a collection of elements of the same type, stored in contiguous memory locations.
- **Types**: MQL5 supports both single-dimensional and multi-dimensional arrays.
- **Dynamic Arrays**: Their size can change during program execution, offering flexibility.

Using Arrays:

- Declaration: **double prices[];** declares an array of doubles.
- Initialization: Arrays can be initialized using an initializer list, e.g., **int numbers[3] = {10, 20, 30};**.
- Accessing Elements: Use the index to access or modify elements, e.g., **prices[0] = 1.234;**.

Structures in MQL5:

- **Definition**: A structure is a user-defined data type that allows the combination of data items of different types.
- **Usage**: Ideal for grouping related data together.

Defining and Using Structures:

- Declaration: **struct TradeInfo { string symbol; double openPrice; int volume; };**
- Creating Instances: **TradeInfo trade;**
- Accessing Members: **trade.symbol = "EURUSD";**

String Manipulation

Working with Strings:

- Strings in MQL5 are represented as arrays of characters.
- MQL5 provides a range of functions for string manipulation, such as `StringLen()`, `StringConcatenate()`, `StringFind()`, `StringSubstr()`, and more.

String Operations:

- Concatenation: `string fullName = StringConcatenate("John ", "Doe");`
- Comparison: Use `StringCompare()` to compare two strings.
- Finding Substrings: `int pos = StringFind(fullName, "Doe");`

Example Code: Array-Based Data Handling

Objective:

- Create a script that uses arrays to store and process a list of currency pairs and their respective last traded prices.

Example Script:

```
void OnStart()
{
    // Declare an array of currency pairs and their prices
    string currencyPairs[] = {"EURUSD", "GBPUSD", "USDJPY"};
    double lastPrices[3];


    // Populate the prices array
    for (int i = 0; i < ArraySize(currencyPairs); i++)
    {
        lastPrices[i] = SymbolInfoDouble(currencyPairs[i], SYMBOL_LAST);
    }
```

```
// Display the currency pairs and their last prices

for (int i = 0; i < ArraySize(currencyPairs); i++)

{

    Print(currencyPairs[i], ": ", lastPrices[i]);

}

}
```

Explanation:

- The script initializes an array **currencyPairs** with a list of currency symbols.
- It then declares a **lastPrices** array to store the latest prices for these pairs.
- Using a loop, the script populates **lastPrices** with the current market prices.
- Finally, it prints each currency pair with its corresponding last traded price.

This chapter provides insights into utilizing advanced data types and collections in MQL5. By mastering arrays, structures, and string manipulation, traders can develop more dynamic, data-driven algorithms. This example illustrates how these data types can be effectively used in real-world scenarios, such as monitoring and analyzing multiple currency pairs simultaneously. Understanding these concepts is vital for advanced MQL5 programming and developing sophisticated trading strategies.

Chapter 8: Object-Oriented Programming in MQL5

Object-Oriented Programming (OOP) is a fundamental programming paradigm that organizes software design around data, or objects, rather than functions and logic. In MQL5, OOP principles enhance the capability to build scalable, efficient, and robust trading systems. This chapter introduces the concepts of classes, objects, inheritance, and encapsulation in MQL5, culminating with an example of creating a basic trading class.

Classes and Objects

Understanding Classes and Objects:

- **Classes**: A class in MQL5 is a blueprint for creating objects (instances). It encapsulates data for the object and methods to manipulate that data.
- **Objects**: An instance of a class. Each object has its own set of data attributes and methods.

Defining a Class:

- Classes are defined with the `class` keyword, followed by data members (variables) and member functions (methods).

    Syntax

```
class ClassName
{
    // Data members
    private:
        double attribute1;
    public:
        void MethodName(); // Member function
};
```

Creating and Using Objects:

- Once a class is defined, objects of that class can be created and used.

    Example:

    ```
    ClassName obj;
    obj.MethodName();
    ```

Inheritance and Encapsulation

Inheritance in MQL5:

- Inheritance allows a new class (derived class) to inherit attributes and methods from an existing class (base class).
- Enhances code reusability and simplifies maintenance.

Encapsulation:

- Encapsulation is the mechanism of restricting direct access to some of an object's components.
- Achieved using access specifiers: **private**, **protected**, and **public**.
- Ensures that object data is hidden from the outside, accessible only through methods.

Example Code: Creating a Basic Trading Class

Objective:

- Develop a basic trading class that encapsulates the logic for placing trades.

Example Script:

```
class BasicTrader
{
   private:
      double entryPrice;
      double lotSize;

   public:
      // Constructor
      BasicTrader(double price, double lot)
      {
        entryPrice = price;
        lotSize = lot;
      }

      // Method to place a buy order
      void PlaceBuyOrder()
      {
          Print("Placing buy order at price: ", entryPrice);
// OrderSend logic here
      }

      // Method to place a sell order
      void PlaceSellOrder()
      {
          Print("Placing sell order at price: ", entryPrice);
          // OrderSend logic here
      }
};
```

```
// Using the BasicTrader class
void OnStart()
{
    BasicTrader trader(1.1350, 0.1);
    trader.PlaceBuyOrder();
    trader.PlaceSellOrder();
}
```

Explanation:

- The **BasicTrader** class encapsulates properties like **entryPrice** and **lotSize**, and methods **PlaceBuyOrder** and **PlaceSellOrder**.
- The class constructor initializes the object with specific values.

- The methods encapsulate the logic for order placement, demonstrating how trading actions can be modularized into a class structure.

In this chapter I introduced the core concepts of OOP in MQL5, an essential programming paradigm for building sophisticated and maintainable trading systems. By utilizing classes, inheritance, and encapsulation, MQL5 programmers can create more organized, reusable, and scalable code, as illustrated in the provided example of a basic trading class. Understanding these OOP principles is vital for any developer looking to advance their skills in MQL5 programming.

Chapter 9: Graphical Objects and User Interface

Creating visually appealing and informative graphical elements is a vital aspect of developing comprehensive trading tools in MQL5. This chapter explores the functionalities for drawing on charts and constructing custom user interfaces, enhancing the interactivity and usability of trading applications. We will also illustrate these concepts with an example of implementing a custom indicator display.

Drawing on Charts

Graphical Objects in MQL5:

- MQL5 provides a rich set of graphical objects like lines, shapes, text, and buttons that can be drawn on charts.
- These objects are used for marking, annotation, and creating custom technical analysis tools.

Types of Graphical Objects:

1. **Simple Objects**: Lines, arrows, and text labels.
2. **Complex Objects**: Fibonacci tools, channels, Gann tools.
3. **Interactive Objects**: Buttons, input fields.

Creating Graphical Objects:

- Use specific functions like `ObjectCreate()`, `ObjectSetText()`, `ObjectSetInteger()`, etc., to create and customize graphical objects.
- Objects can be static or dynamically updated based on price data or other conditions.

Creating Custom Interfaces

Custom Interfaces in MT5:

- Beyond charting, MQL5 allows for the creation of custom panels and interfaces, enhancing user interaction.
- This includes custom settings panels, information dashboards, and interactive control elements.

Building a Custom Interface:

- Utilize MQL5's native functions to create forms, controls, and event handlers.
- Interface elements can be made interactive with the use of event handling functions like **OnChartEvent()**.

Design Considerations:

- Ensure interfaces are intuitive and user-friendly.
- Consider the visual appeal and readability of your interface elements.

Example Code: Implementing a Custom Indicator Display

Objective:

- Develop a simple custom indicator that displays the current price and a moving average on the chart.

Example Script

```
input int maPeriod = 14; // Period for Moving Average




//-------------------------------------------------------------------

//| Custom indicator initialization function             |

//-------------------------------------------------------------------

void OnInit()

{

  // Create a label to display the price

  ObjectCreate(0, "PriceLabel", OBJ_LABEL, 0, 0, 0);

  ObjectSetInteger(0, "PriceLabel", OBJPROP_CORNER, CORNER_RIGHT_UPPER);

  ObjectSetInteger(0, "PriceLabel", OBJPROP_XDISTANCE, 10);
```

```
    ObjectSetInteger(0, "PriceLabel", OBJPROP_YDISTANCE, 10);


    // Create a label to display the moving average
    ObjectCreate(0, "MALabel", OBJ_LABEL, 0, 0, 0);
    ObjectSetInteger(0, "MALabel", OBJPROP_CORNER, CORNER_RIGHT_UPPER);
    ObjectSetInteger(0, "MALabel", OBJPROP_XDISTANCE, 10);
    ObjectSetInteger(0, "MALabel", OBJPROP_YDISTANCE, 30);
}


//-------------------------------------------------------------------------
//| Custom indicator iteration function                          |
//-------------------------------------------------------------------------
void OnCalculate(const int rates_total,
        const int prev_calculated,
        const datetime &time[],
        const double &open[],
        const double &high[],
        const double &low[],
        const double &close[],
        const long &tick_volume[],
        const long &volume[],
        const int &spread[])
```

```
{
    // Update price label

    double price = close[0];

    ObjectSetText("PriceLabel", "Current Price: " + DoubleToString(price, _Digits));


    // Update moving average label

    double ma = iMA(_Symbol, _Period, maPeriod, 0, MODE_SMA, PRICE_CLOSE, 0);

    ObjectSetText("MALabel", "MA(" + IntegerToString(maPeriod) + "): " +
    DoubleToString(ma, _Digits));

}
```

Explanation:

- The `OnInit()` function creates two labels for displaying the current price and moving average (MA).

- The labels are positioned in the upper right corner of the chart.

- The `OnCalculate()` function is triggered on every new tick and updates the labels with the latest price and MA value.

This chapter has provided insights into the graphical capabilities of MQL5, essential for enhancing the visual appeal and functionality of trading tools. By utilizing graphical objects and custom interfaces, developers can create more interactive and informative trading applications. This example demonstrates how these elements can be effectively used to display real-time data, a fundamental requirement in most trading scenarios. Understanding these graphical features is crucial for any trader or developer looking to build advanced tools in MetaTrader 5.

Chapter 10: Working with Indicators and Technical Analysis

Technical indicators are crucial tools in trading, providing insights into market trends, volatility, momentum, and various other aspects of financial markets. MQL5, the programming language used in MetaTrader 5 (MT5), offers extensive capabilities for utilizing built-in indicators and developing custom ones. This chapter delves into how to leverage these indicators for technical analysis and includes an example of writing a moving average crossover indicator.

Overview:

- MT5 comes with a wide range of built-in indicators like Moving Averages, Bollinger Bands, MACD, RSI, and many others.

- These indicators can be accessed directly from the MT5 interface or used programmatically in MQL5 scripts.

Using Built-in Indicators

- **Through MT5 Interface**: Drag and drop the desired indicator onto a chart.
- **Via MQL5**: Use indicator functions like **iMA()**, **iBands()**, **iMACD()**, etc., in your scripts.

Example of Using a Built-in Indicator in MQL5:

```
double ma = iMA(_Symbol, _Period, 14, 0, MODE_SMA, PRICE_CLOSE, 0);
```

This line of code calculates the Simple Moving Average (SMA) for the current symbol and period.

Developing Custom Indicators

Creating Your Own Indicators:

- MQL5 allows traders and developers to create their own custom indicators.
- Custom indicators can be tailored to specific trading strategies or analytical methods.

Key Steps:

1. **Define the Indicator**: Start by defining what your indicator will measure or signal.
2. **Coding**: Use MQL5 to program the indicator logic. This involves calculations based on price data or other indicators.
3. **Visualization**: Decide how the indicator will be displayed on the chart. This could be lines, histograms, dots, etc.

Testing and Optimization:

- Test the custom indicator thoroughly to ensure it works as expected.
- Optimize its parameters for different instruments or market conditions.

Example Code: Writing a Moving Average Crossover Indicator

Objective:

- Develop a custom indicator that signals a crossover between two moving averages, a common technical analysis strategy.

Example Script

```
#property indicator_chart_window
#property indicator_buffers 2
#property indicator_color1 Blue
#property indicator_color2 Red

double fastMA[];
double slowMA[];

int OnInit()
{
    SetIndexBuffer(0, fastMA);
    SetIndexBuffer(1, slowMA);

    return(INIT_SUCCEEDED);
}

void OnCalculate(const int rates_total,
            const int prev_calculated,
            const datetime &time[],
            const double &open[],
```

```
            const double &high[],

            const double &low[],

            const double &close[],

            const long &tick_volume[],

            const long &volume[],

            const int &spread[])


    int fastMAPeriod = 10;

    int slowMAPeriod = 20;


    for(int i = 0; i < rates_total; i++)
    {
        fastMA[i] = iMA(_Symbol, _Period, fastMAPeriod, 0, MODE_SMA, PRICE_CLOSE, i);

        slowMA[i] = iMA(_Symbol, _Period, slowMAPeriod, 0, MODE_SMA, PRICE_CLOSE, i);

    }

}
```

Explanation:

- The indicator has two buffers, **fastMA** and **slowMA**, representing the values of the fast and slow moving averages.
- **SetIndexBuffer()** associates each buffer with a line on the chart.
- In **OnCalculate()**, the indicator calculates the values of the two moving averages for each bar.
- The indicator plots two lines on the chart, allowing traders to visually identify crossovers.

In this chapter, we have explored how to use and develop indicators in MQL5, essential for technical analysis in trading. With the provided example demonstrates the creation of a custom moving average crossover indicator, a popular tool in trading strategy development. Mastering the use of indicators is crucial for traders and developers looking to build advanced analytical tools in MT5.

Chapter 11: Price and Order Data

Effective trading strategies in MetaTrader 5 (MT5) hinge on a comprehensive understanding of price data and the nuances of order placement. This chapter focuses on the different types of orders available in MT5, how to access and interpret price data, and concludes with a practical example of a function for placing orders.

Understanding Order Types

Different Order Types in MT5:

1. **Market Orders**: Orders executed immediately at the current market price. Includes 'Buy' (to go long) and 'Sell' (to go short) orders.

2. **Pending Orders**: Orders to buy or sell at a pre-defined price in the future. Types include:

   - **Buy Limit**: Buy when the market price drops to a specified level.
   - **Sell Limit**: Sell when the market price rises to a specified level.
   - **Buy Stop**: Buy when the market price rises to a specified level.
   - **Sell Stop**: Sell when the market price drops to a specified level.

3. **Stop Loss and Take Profit**: Orders set to close a trade at a particular price level to minimize losses (Stop Loss) or lock in profits (Take Profit).

Choosing the Right Order Type:

- Selection depends on the trading strategy, market conditions, and risk management practices.

Accessing Price Data

Retrieving Price Information:

- **Market Information Functions**: MT5 provides functions like **SymbolInfoDouble()**, **SymbolInfoTick()**, and **MarketInfo()** to retrieve current market prices and other related data.

Example - Getting the Current Bid and Ask Prices:

```
double askPrice = SymbolInfoDouble(_Symbol, SYMBOL_ASK);

double bidPrice = SymbolInfoDouble(_Symbol, SYMBOL_BID);

Print("Ask Price: ", askPrice, " Bid Price: ", bidPrice);
```

Example Code: Order Placement Function

Objective:

- Develop a function to place different types of orders based on input parameters.

Example Script:

```
// Function to place an order
bool PlaceTrade(string symbol, ENUM_ORDER_TYPE type, double volume, double price,
double sl, double tp, string comment)
{
    MqlTradeRequest request;
    MqlTradeResult result;

    // Set common parameters
    request.symbol = symbol;
    request.volume = volume;
```

```
    request.comment = comment;
request.sl = sl;
    request.tp = tp;

    // Set parameters based on order type
    switch(type)
    {
        case ORDER_TYPE_BUY:
            request.action = TRADE_ACTION_DEAL;
            request.type = ORDER_TYPE_BUY;
            request.price = SymbolInfoDouble(symbol, SYMBOL_ASK);
            break;

        case ORDER_TYPE_SELL:
            request.action = TRADE_ACTION_DEAL;
            request.type = ORDER_TYPE_SELL;
            request.price = SymbolInfoDouble(symbol, SYMBOL_BID);
            break;

        // Add cases for pending orders (Buy Limit, Sell Limit, etc.)
    }

    // Send the order
    return OrderSend(request, result);
}

// Example usage
```

```
void OnStart()

{

    if(!PlaceTrade("EURUSD", ORDER_TYPE_BUY, 0.1, 0.0, 0.0, 0.0, "My EA Order"))

    {

        Print("Order placement failed!");

    }

}
```

Explanation:

- `PlaceTrade` function handles the placement of different order types.
- `MqlTradeRequest` and `MqlTradeResult` structures are used to define the order and handle the result.
- The function adjusts parameters based on the type of order (market or pending).
- The `OrderSend()` function is used to send the order to the broker.
- An example usage demonstrates placing a buy order for EURUSD.

In this chapter, we have covered the essentials of understanding and working with price and order data in MQL5. Mastery of these concepts is vital for developing effective trading strategies and automated trading systems in MT5. The example illustrates a practical approach to placing various types of orders, a fundamental skill for any trader or developer in the MT5 environment.

Chapter 12: Trade Operations and Management

Effective trade management is critical in the world of automated trading, particularly when using MetaTrader 5 (MT5). This chapter focuses on essential techniques for managing trades and orders in MQL5, along with implementing risk management strategies. We'll conclude with an example that demonstrates integrating risk parameters into a trade management system.

Managing Trades and Orders

Trade and Order Functions:

- MT5 offers various functions to manage trades and orders, like **OrderSend()**, **OrderModify()**, and **OrderClose()**.

- Understanding these functions is key to controlling open positions and pending orders.

Monitoring Open Trades:

- Use **PositionsTotal()**, **PositionGetTicket()**, and related functions to monitor and manage open positions.

- Handling different trade conditions and responses is crucial for adapting to market changes.

Modifying and Closing Orders:

- Modify orders to adjust Stop Loss (SL) and Take Profit (TP) levels using **OrderModify()**.

- Close orders either partially or fully depending on the strategy and market conditions.

Risk Management Techniques

Importance of Risk Management:

- Proper risk management is essential to protect capital and ensure long-term trading sustainability.

- It involves setting predefined rules for trade sizes, SL, TP, and overall exposure.

Common Risk Management Strategies:

1. **Setting Stop Loss and Take Profit**: Crucial for limiting losses and securing profits.

2. **Position Sizing**: Determining the appropriate trade size based on account balance and risk tolerance.

3. **Risk-Reward Ratio**: Establishing a ratio to balance potential profits against potential losses.

4. **Diversification**: Reducing risk by spreading trades across different instruments or strategies.

Example Code: Trade Manager with Risk Parameters

Objective:

- Create a simple trade manager function that incorporates basic risk management parameters.

Example Script

```
// Trade manager function with risk management

bool ManageTrade(string symbol, double riskPercent, double riskRewardRatio)

{

    double accountBalance = AccountBalance();

    double riskAmount = accountBalance * riskPercent / 100.0;

    double stopLossPips = 20; // Example SL in pips

    double lotSize = riskAmount / (stopLossPips * _Point / SymbolInfoDouble(symbol,
SYMBOL_TRADE_TICK_VALUE));

    double takeProfitPips = stopLossPips * riskRewardRatio;


    // Place the trade with calculated lot size, SL, and TP

    MqlTradeRequest request;
```

```mql
    MqlTradeResult result;


    request.action = TRADE_ACTION_DEAL;

    request.symbol = symbol;

    request.volume = lotSize;

    request.type = ORDER_TYPE_BUY; // Example for a buy order

    request.price = SymbolInfoDouble(symbol, SYMBOL_ASK);

    request.sl = request.price - stopLossPips * _Point;

    request.tp = request.price + takeProfitPips * _Point;


    return OrderSend(request, result);
}
// Example usage
void OnStart()
{
    if(!ManageTrade("EURUSD", 1.0, 2.0))
    {
        Print("Trade placement failed!");
    }
}
```

Explanation:

- The **ManageTrade** function calculates the lot size based on the specified risk percentage and the risk-reward ratio.
- It sets the SL and TP levels according to the given parameters.
- The function then sends a buy order (as an example) with the calculated lot size, SL, and TP.
- It demonstrates a simple but effective approach to integrating risk management into trade execution.

In this chapter, we have explored the essentials of trade operations and risk management in MQL5. Effective trade management and adherence to disciplined risk management strategies are paramount for success in automated trading. The example serves as a basic framework for a trade manager that incorporates fundamental risk parameters, illustrating how risk management can be integrated into automated trading systems.

Chapter 13: Error Handling and Debugging

Effective error handling and debugging are crucial for developing robust and reliable trading applications in MQL5. This chapter focuses on strategies for catching and handling errors and outlines various debugging techniques. Additionally, we'll provide an example demonstrating robust error handling in trade operations, ensuring smoother execution and enhanced reliability of your MQL5 scripts.

Catching and Handling Errors

Importance of Error Handling:

- Error handling in MQL5 is essential to manage and respond to issues that arise during the execution of a script, particularly in live trading environments.

Common Error Handling Techniques:

1. **Try-Catch Blocks**: Although traditional try-catch blocks are not available in MQL5, similar functionality can be achieved using conditional checks after operation calls.
2. **Error Codes**: MQL5 functions often return specific error codes which can be used to identify and handle different types of errors.

Interpreting Error Codes:

- Use the **GetLastError()** function immediately after a trade function call to get the error code.
- Refer to MQL5 documentation for a detailed description of error codes.

Debugging Techniques in MQL5

Debugging Tools:

- **MetaEditor**: Integrated development environment (IDE) with features like breakpoints, step execution, and variable watches.

- **Print Statements**: Use **Print()** function to output values to the logs for debugging purposes.

Strategies for Effective Debugging:

1. **Break Down the Code**: Test small parts of your code independently to isolate the error.

2. **Check for Logical Errors**: Look for mistakes in the logic that might not throw explicit errors but result in incorrect behavior.

3. **Use the Strategy Tester**: Simulate your script in different market conditions to test its reliability and performance.

Example Code: Robust Error Handling in Trade Operations

Objective:

- Implement error handling in a function that executes a trade, managing different error scenarios effectively.

Example Script

```
bool PlaceOrderWithErrorHandling()
{
  MqlTradeRequest request;
  MqlTradeResult result;


  request.action = TRADE_ACTION_DEAL;
  request.symbol = _Symbol;
  request.volume = 0.1;  // Example volume
  request.type = ORDER_TYPE_BUY;  // Example order type
  request.price = SymbolInfoDouble(_Symbol, SYMBOL_ASK);


  // Send the order
  if(!OrderSend(request, result))
  {
    int errorCode = GetLastError();
```

```
        Print("OrderSend failed with error code: ", errorCode);


        // Handle specific errors
        switch(errorCode)
        {
           case ERR_INVALID_TRADE_PARAMETERS:
              Print("Invalid trade parameters.");
              break;
           case ERR_SERVER_BUSY:
              Print("Trade server is busy.");
              break;
           // Add cases for other relevant errors
        }
        return false;
    }
    Print("Order placed successfully. Ticket: ", result.order);
    return true;
}
// Example usage
void OnStart()
{
   if(!PlaceOrderWithErrorHandling())
   {
      Print("Trade execution failed.");
   }
}
```

Explanation:

- The function **PlaceOrderWithErrorHandling** attempts to place a trade order and checks for errors if the **OrderSend** function fails.

- The **GetLastError()** function retrieves the error code, which is then used to provide specific feedback and handle known error scenarios.

- This example demonstrates a proactive approach to handling potential issues during trade execution, making the script more robust and reliable.

In this chapter, we've covered the essential aspects of error handling and debugging in MQL5. The ability to effectively catch, handle, and debug errors is crucial for the development of reliable and efficient automated trading systems. The example serves as a practical guide to implementing robust error handling in your MQL5 scripts, ensuring better stability and performance in real-world trading scenarios.

Chapter 14: Strategy Development and Backtesting

Developing a successful trading strategy and rigorously backtesting it are fundamental steps in automated trading using MQL5. This chapter provides insights into the process of creating a trading strategy, followed by thorough backtesting and optimization to validate its effectiveness. We conclude with an example script demonstrating how to backtest a strategy in MetaTrader 5 (MT5).

Developing a Trading Strategy

Key Elements of a Trading Strategy:

1. **Market Conditions**: Identify the market conditions under which the strategy should operate (e.g., trending, range-bound markets).

2. **Entry and Exit Criteria**: Define clear rules for when to enter and exit trades. This may include technical indicators, price patterns, or economic events.

3. **Risk Management**: Establish rules for managing risk, including setting stop-loss and take-profit levels, position sizing, and maximum drawdown.

4. **Timeframe**: Decide on the timeframe that the strategy will operate in (e.g., intraday, daily).

Considerations in Strategy Development:

- **Simplicity vs. Complexity**: Strive for a balance between a simple, understandable strategy and incorporating sufficient complexity to capture market dynamics.

- **Historical Data Analysis**: Analyze historical price data to gain insights and refine strategy parameters.

- **Adaptability**: Ensure the strategy is adaptable to different market conditions.

Backtesting and Optimization

Purpose of Backtesting:

- Backtesting involves running the strategy against historical data to evaluate its performance and robustness.

Backtesting in MT5:

- Use the built-in Strategy Tester in MT5 for backtesting. It provides detailed reports on the strategy's performance, including profitability, drawdown, and trade statistics.

Optimization:

- Optimization is the process of fine-tuning the strategy parameters to improve performance.
- MT5's Strategy Tester can also perform optimization by testing various combinations of parameters.

Key Metrics:

- Pay attention to metrics like total net profit, profit factor, maximum drawdown, and the Sharpe ratio.

Example Code: Strategy Backtesting Script

Objective:

- Create a basic backtesting script in MQL5 for a Moving Average Crossover strategy.

Example Script

```
input int fastMAPeriod = 10; // Fast Moving Average Period

input int slowMAPeriod = 20; // Slow Moving Average Period


//-------------------------------------------------------------------
// Expert initialization function                    |
//-------------------------------------------------------------------
```

```
int OnInit()
{
    // Set up the indicator buffers
    SetIndexBuffer(0, fastMA);
    SetIndexBuffer(1, slowMA);
    return(INIT_SUCCEEDED);
}
//-----------------------------------------------------------------------
// Expert tick function                          |
//-----------------------------------------------------------------------
void OnTick()
{
    // Calculate Moving Averages
double fastMA = iMA(_Symbol, _Period, fastMAPeriod, 0, MODE_SMA, PRICE_CLOSE, 0);
double slowMA = iMA(_Symbol, _Period, slowMAPeriod, 0, MODE_SMA, PRICE_CLOSE, 0);

    // Check for crossover and open trades accordingly
    if(fastMA > slowMA && OrdersTotal() == 0)
    {
        // Open a buy order
    }
    else if(fastMA < slowMA && OrdersTotal() == 0)
    {
        // Open a sell order
    }
}
```

Chapter 15: Working with Events and Notifications

Event-driven programming combined with efficient notification systems is essential in automated trading, especially within the MetaTrader 5 (MT5) platform. This chapter delves into the fundamentals of event-driven programming in MQL5, the configuration and implementation of various notification types, and provides an illustrative example of integrating email and mobile notifications into a trading script.

Event-Driven Programming in MQL5

Fundamentals of Event-Driven Programming:

- Event-driven programming is a paradigm in which the flow of the program is determined by events such as user actions, sensor outputs, or message passing.
- In MQL5, this primarily involves responding to market events, user inputs, or predefined conditions.

Common Event Handlers in MQL5:

- **OnTick()**: This handler is invoked on every new tick data, crucial for real-time trading decisions.

- **OnTimer()**: Used for operations that need to be executed periodically, not necessarily on every tick.

- **OnChartEvent()**: Handles user interactions with the chart interface, useful for creating interactive custom indicators or EAs.

- **OnTrade()**: Responds to changes in trade positions, like the opening or closing of trades.

Setting Up Notifications and Alerts

Email and Mobile Notifications:

- MQL5 offers functions to send email (**SendMail**) and mobile notifications (**SendNotification**).

- These functions allow traders to get immediate alerts about significant events or conditions in their trading environment.

Configuring MT5 for Notifications:

- **Email Setup**: Configure SMTP server details in MT5 options under the "Email" tab. This requires SMTP server, SMTP login, and SMTP password.

- **Mobile Notifications**: Set up by specifying the MetaQuotes ID in the MT5 options under the "Notifications" tab. The MetaQuotes ID is available in the mobile MT5 app settings.

Example Code: Email and Mobile Notifications

Objective:

- Implement a function in MQL5 that triggers email and mobile notifications upon a specific trading event, such as the execution of a trade.

Example Script:

```
void TriggerNotifications(string eventDetails)

{

    string emailSubject = "MT5 Alert: " + eventDetails;

    string emailBody = "Alert Details: " + eventDetails + ". Check your MT5 platform for
more info.";

    // Sending an email notification

    if(!SendMail(emailSubject, emailBody))

    {

        Print("Email notification failed. Error: ", GetLastError());

    }

    // Sending a mobile notification

    if(!SendNotification("MT5 Mobile Alert: " + eventDetails))

    {

        Print("Mobile notification failed. Error: ", GetLastError());

    }

}

// Usage example in a trade event scenario

void OnTrade()

{

    // Assuming a function that checks a certain trade condition

    if(CheckTradeCondition())

    {

        TriggerNotifications("New trade executed");

    }

}
```

Explanation:

- **TriggerNotifications** is a custom function that takes a string detailing the event.

- It uses **SendMail** for email alerts, where **emailSubject** and **emailBody** contain the email's content. The SMTP settings must be pre-configured in MT5.

- **SendNotification** is used for sending alerts to a mobile device. The MetaQuotes ID should be set in MT5 to use this feature.

- The **OnTrade** event handler illustrates an example use case, where the function is called when a specific trade condition is met.

In this chapter, we have covered how to effectively use event-driven programming and set up vital notifications in MQL5. By integrating these functionalities into your trading scripts, you can stay updated with real-time events and make informed decisions promptly. The provided example demonstrates a implementation of both email and mobile notifications, which are indispensable tools for modern traders leveraging automated systems.

Chapter 16: Integration with External Data and Services

In the realm of automated trading, the ability to integrate with external data sources and services greatly enhances the capabilities of trading systems. This chapter focuses on the methods for utilizing web requests and interfacing with databases in MQL5. We will also provide an example demonstrating how to fetch external economic data, which can be pivotal for informed trading decisions.

Using Web Requests

Overview of Web Requests in MQL5:

- Web requests in MQL5 allow scripts to interact with external servers via HTTP/HTTPS, enabling access to various online data sources and services.

- This feature can be used to get real-time financial news, economic event data, or even interact with custom web-based APIs.

Setting Up for Web Requests:

- **Allowing Web Requests**: In MT5, go to 'Tools' -> 'Options' -> 'Expert Advisors'. Check the box next to 'Allow WebRequest for listed URL'.

- **Specifying URLs**: Add the URLs you will be accessing to the list. Only these URLs will be accessible via the script.

Using the WebRequest Function:

- The **WebRequest** function in MQL5 is used to send and receive data from specified URLs.

- It requires parameters like the URL, request headers, post data, and a container to receive the response data.

Interfacing with Databases

Database Connectivity in MQL5:

- While MQL5 does not provide direct database connectivity features, it can interface with databases using external DLLs or through web service APIs.

- This functionality is useful for storing trading data, accessing historical data, or integrating with custom data analytics tools.

Creating a Database Connection:

- **Via External DLLs**: Use MQL5's ability to call functions from DLLs to interact with a database.

- **Via Web API**: Design a web service API that interfaces with your database and interact with this API using MQL5 web requests.

Example Code: Fetching External Economic Data

Objective:

- Write a script in MQL5 to fetch economic calendar data from an external web service.

Example Script

```
string url = "https://api.example.com/economic_calendar"; // Example API endpoint

char post[], result[];

char headers[] = "Content-Type: application/x-www-form-urlencoded\r\n";


void OnStart()

{

  // Setting up for a WebRequest
```

```
    int timeout = 30;

    int httpResponseCode;

    string httpResponseHeader;


    // Send the WebRequest

    if(WebRequest("GET", url, headers, timeout, post, result, httpResponseCode,
httpResponseHeader) == -1)

    {

        Print("WebRequest failed. Error code: ", GetLastError());

        return;

    }


    // Process the received data

    string economicData = CharArrayToString(result);

    Print("Received Economic Data: ", economicData);


    // Further data processing and integration into trading logic

}
```

Explanation:

- The script uses the **WebRequest** function to send an HTTP GET request to an economic calendar API.
- The response is received in a character array and converted into a string for further processing.
- Error handling is implemented to catch any issues with the request.
- The received data can then be integrated into the trading system for strategy refinement or decision-making.

In this chapter, we have explored how MQL5 can be used to extend the functionalities of trading systems by integrating with external data and services. Web requests and database interfacing, MQL5 scripts can access a vast array of external resources, significantly enhancing the analytical and operational capabilities of automated trading systems. The example provided illustrates a practical application of fetching external economic data, showcasing the potential of MQL5 in leveraging external data sources.

Chapter 17: Building a Real-World Automated Trading Bot

The culmination of mastering MQL5 is the ability to build a comprehensive, real-world automated trading bot. This chapter brings together the concepts covered in previous chapters, focusing on the development of a complete trading bot that integrates a trading strategy with risk management features. We'll provide an example of such a bot, highlighting key areas like strategy implementation, order management, and risk control.

Consolidating Learned Concepts

Integrating Core Concepts:

- A sophisticated trading bot in MQL5 should effectively integrate various aspects such as event-driven programming, working with indicators, managing orders, and error handling.

- The bot should be able to analyze market data, execute trades based on a defined strategy, and manage those trades in line with risk parameters.

Developing a Comprehensive Trading Bot

Key Components of the Trading Bot:

1. **Market Analysis**: Utilize technical indicators and price data to analyze the market and generate trading signals.

2. **Order Execution**: Implement logic to place and manage trades based on the signals generated.

3. **Risk Management**: Include features to control risk, such as setting stop-loss orders, managing position sizes, and defining maximum drawdown limits.

Design Considerations:

- **Reliability and Efficiency**: The bot should execute operations swiftly and reliably, handling errors and unexpected market conditions effectively.

- **Adaptability**: It should be adaptable to different market environments and be easily tunable for different assets or trading styles.

Example Code: A Complete Trading Bot with Strategy and Risk Management

Objective:

- Develop an automated trading bot that uses a simple moving average crossover strategy and includes basic risk management features.

Example Script

```
input int fastMAPeriod = 10;

input int slowMAPeriod = 20;

input double riskPerTrade = 0.02; // Risk 2% of account balance per trade

input double maxDrawdown = 0.20; // Maximum drawdown limit 20%

double accountMaxBalance; // To track the maximum account balance


int OnInit()

{

    accountMaxBalance = AccountBalance();

    return(INIT_SUCCEEDED);

}

void OnTick()

{

    // Check for drawdown limit

    if(AccountBalance() < accountMaxBalance * (1 - maxDrawdown))

    {

        // Implement logic to pause trading or close positions

        return;

    }

    // Update maximum account balance
```

```
accountMaxBalance = MathMax(accountMaxBalance, AccountBalance());

// Strategy logic - Moving Average Crossover
double fastMA = iMA(_Symbol, _Period, fastMAPeriod, 0, MODE_SMA, PRICE_CLOSE,
0);

double slowMA = iMA(_Symbol, _Period, slowMAPeriod, 0, MODE_SMA, PRICE_CLOSE,
0);

if(fastMA > slowMA && OrdersTotal() == 0)
{
    // Buy logic
    double lotSize = CalculateLotSize(riskPerTrade);
    // Place buy order with calculated lot size
}
else if(fastMA < slowMA && OrdersTotal() == 0)
{
    // Sell logic
    double lotSize = CalculateLotSize(riskPerTrade);
    // Place sell order with calculated lot size
}
}
double CalculateLotSize(double riskPercent)
{
    // Calculate the lot size based on account balance and risk per trade
    // ...
    return lotSize;
}
```

Explanation:

- The bot uses a moving average crossover strategy to generate trading signals.

- Risk management is handled by checking the account's drawdown and adjusting the lot size based on the risk per trade.

- **CalculateLotSize** is a placeholder function where the actual calculation would depend on the account balance, stop-loss size, and risk percentage.

- The bot updates the maximum account balance to track drawdown.

This chapter provides a framework for building a real-world automated trading bot in MQL5, integrating strategy development, risk management, and practical trading functions. The provided example is a foundation upon which further complexity and features can be added, tailored to specific trading goals and risk profiles. Developing such a bot not only requires technical proficiency in MQL5 but also a deep understanding of trading principles and risk management strategies.

Chapter 18: Best Practices and Moving Forward

As we conclude our exploration of MQL5 programming for automated trading, it's essential to focus on best practices that ensure the creation of efficient, reliable, and maintainable trading bots. This chapter outlines these practices, discusses the importance of staying updated with market changes, and looks at future trends in automated trading.

Best Practices in MQL5 Programming

Code Organization and Readability:

- **Modular Design**: Write modular code with functions and classes to improve readability and maintainability.

- **Comments and Documentation**: Thoroughly comment on your code and maintain documentation for complex logic or strategies.

Error Handling:

- Implement comprehensive error handling to catch and respond to runtime errors, especially in trade execution functions.

Efficient Use of Resources:

- Optimize your code to use resources efficiently, particularly important in high-frequency trading bots.
- Avoid unnecessary calculations or loops within frequently called functions like **OnTick()**.

Testing and Optimization:

- Regularly backtest and optimize your trading strategies under different market conditions.
- Use MT5's Strategy Tester for historical backtesting and to simulate various scenarios.

Version Control:

- Use version control systems like Git to track changes, manage different versions of your scripts, and collaborate with others.

Staying Updated with Market Changes

Continuous Learning:

- Markets evolve, and so should your trading strategies. Stay informed about financial markets, economic events, and new trading theories or techniques.
- Regularly review and adjust your trading algorithms based on market performance and changing dynamics.

Incorporating Market Feedback:

- Use market feedback to refine your strategies. Monitor the performance of your bots and analyze any shortcomings or areas for improvement.

Economic and Financial Updates:

- Keep an eye on economic calendars, financial news, and market analyses. These can provide valuable insights that may impact your trading strategies.

Future Trends in Automated Trading

Emerging Technologies:

- Explore emerging technologies like machine learning and artificial intelligence, which are becoming increasingly prevalent in trading algorithms.

Regulatory Changes:

- Stay aware of regulatory changes in the financial markets that may affect automated trading practices.

Integration with Other Systems:

- Look into integrating your trading bots with other systems or platforms, enhancing capabilities and access to diverse markets.

Sustainability and Ethical Trading:

- Consider the sustainability and ethical implications of trading strategies, focusing on long-term viability over short-term gains.

Example Code: Incorporating Best Practices

Objective:

- Illustrate a simple code snippet that embodies best practices in MQL5 programming.

Example Script

```
// Example MQL5 script implementing best practices

input double riskPerTrade = 0.02; // Example risk per trade parameter

//------------------------------------------------------------------
//| Expert initialization function                        |
//------------------------------------------------------------------
int OnInit()
{
    // Initialization logic
    // ...
    return(INIT_SUCCEEDED);
}


//------------------------------------------------------------------
//| Main trading logic in the OnTick function             |
//------------------------------------------------------------------
void OnTick()
{
    // Market analysis logic
    // ...
```

```
    // Trade execution with error handling
    if(ShouldExecuteTrade())
    {
        if(!ExecuteTrade(riskPerTrade))
        {
            Print("Trade execution failed. Error code: ", GetLastError());
        }
    }
}
//-----------------------------------------------------------------------
// Modular function for executing trades
bool ExecuteTrade(double risk)
{
    // Trade execution logic with risk management
    // ...
    return true; // Return true if successful
}


//-----------------------------------------------------------------------
// Utility function to determine if a trade should be executed
bool ShouldExecuteTrade()
{
    // Logic to determine trade execution
    // ...
    return true; // Example condition
}
```

Explanation:

- The script is structured with a clear separation of concerns: initialization, main trading logic, and modular functions for specific tasks.

- It includes risk management considerations and error handling.

- Comments and structured formatting enhance the readability and maintainability of the script.

In conclusion, adhering to best practices in MQL5 programming is vital for the success of automated trading strategies. As the market continues to evolve, staying informed and adaptable is just as important as technical proficiency. Future trends in automated trading promise exciting developments, and staying abreast of these changes will be key to maintaining a competitive edge in the world of algorithmic trading.

No Bulling Around with
MQL5 MetaTrader
Programming

By: Michael Neumann

Published by Mediaguruz Publishing at Mediaguruz.com